Original title:

Roots of Reflection

Copyright © 2024 Taago Leppik

All rights reserved.

Author: Augustus Flowman

ISBN HARDBACK: 978-9916-733-72-1

ISBN PAPERBACK: 978-9916-733-73-8

The Inward Journey

In silence I seek, the depths of my mind,
Whispers of truth in shadows unwind.
A mirror reflects the soul's quiet plea,
To find the lost parts that yearn to be free.

Through valleys of thought, I wander alone,
With each step I take, the essence I've grown.
Guided by stars, in the dark I perceive,
That healing begins when I learn to believe.

The heart's gentle compass points towards the
light,
Illuminating paths hidden from sight.
With courage, I climb through the layers of pain,

Emerging anew, like a dancer in rain.

As I journey within, I gather my voice,
Embracing the silence, I make my choice.
To honor the scars as a part of my fate,

I rise from the ashes, transformed by my weight.

Soil and Soul Intertwined

In the earth's soft embrace, my spirit finds home,

Roots deep in the soil, where the ancients roam.
Seeds of my dreams take flight with the breeze,
Nurtured by rain, and whispered by trees.

The fragrance of life, in every rich hue,
Brings forth the magic, where wonders renew.
From darkness emerges the strength of the bold,
In harmony's dance, stories unfold.

Each tender shoot rises towards the sun's glow,
Reflecting the journeys of all that I know.
In the cycles of nature, I've planted my heart,
For soil and soul thrive, never apart.

In moments of stillness, I listen and feel,
The wisdom of ages, the universe's wheel.
Through struggles and triumphs, we grow side
by side,

In the tapestry woven, our spirits confide.

Footprints in the Soil

On paths where whispers tread,
A journey marked by steps,
Each print a story read,
In earth where silence kept.

The sun casts shadows long,
As memories unfold,
With every stride, a song,
In whispers of the old.

Nature's hand does trace,
The tales of those who roam,
In every mark and space,
The soil becomes our home.

As time erodes away,
The imprint still will stay,
A testament to all,
In footsteps that don't fall.

Echoing Heartbeats

In silence, hearts converse,
With rhythms soft, yet loud,
A symphony diverse,
In shadows of the crowd.

Each pulse a gentle thrum,
Resonating deep within,
A chorus we become,
A song that won't grow dim.

Beneath the stars so bright,
We gather, spirits free,
In echoes of the night,
Our heartbeats join, and see.

United in the beat,
A dance of souls' embrace,
With every thump, we meet,
In this sacred, shared space.

Ties that Bind Us

In the laughter shared, we find our strength,
Through every moment, we go to great lengths.
With hands held tight, we face the storm,
Creating a shelter, where hearts are warm.

From whispers soft, to shouts so loud,
We weave our story, a tapestry proud.
In every tear that falls like rain,
We find the beauty, amidst the pain.

Through seasons' change, we stand as one,
Together we rise, when day is done.
In love and trust, our roots run deep,
The ties that bind, are ours to keep.

In the Shadows of Memory

In the quiet dusk, memories play,
Flickering softly, they drift away.
With every heartbeat, a story unfolds,
In the shadows of time, where silence holds.

Ghosts of laughter linger near,
Whispers from yesteryears, so clear.
Each moment cherished, a fragile thread,
Stitched to the dreams that live in our head.

Though shadows grow long, and daylight fades,
In the depths of dusk, love never evades.
We carry the echoes, of joy and strife,
In the shadows of memory, we find our life.

Levels of Understanding

In the quiet depths of thought,
We gather pieces of the world.
Each layer revealed like secrets,
Unfolding truths that go unheard.

With every question we pursue,
Light breaks through the shadows cast.
Connecting dots of knowledge,
Building bridges to the past.

The layers peel back slowly,
Understanding takes its time.
In the heart of every learning,
Wisdom grows in subtle rhyme.

So let us dive into the deep,
With open hearts and eager minds.
For in the quest for clarity,
The richest treasures we will find.

Traces of the Unknown

Mist wraps the land in silence,
Where secrets linger in the dusk.
Footprints vanish in the shadows,
Leaving traces of their trust.

Whispers float on the cool breeze,
Hints of stories left untold.
Curiosity sparks within,
A yearning for the hidden gold.

The unknown calls to wanderers,
With promises of wonders new.
Every step a leap of faith,
As horizons shift in view.

With wonder as our lantern,
We navigate through the obscure.
For in the dark, there lies a path,
A chance to glean, a chance to explore.

Portraits of the Past

Faded frames with whispers low,
Silent tales that time does sew.
Colors dimmed, yet still they gleam,
Echoes of a long-lost dream.

Eyes that sparkle, hearts that sigh,
Moments captured, drifting by.
Each glance holds a fleeting trace,
Stories written on each face.

In the corners, shadows play,
Memories that refuse to stay.
Hands entwined in gentle grace,
Love reflected in each place.

Time moves on, yet they remain,
Haunting whispers of joy and pain.
In every portrait, a fleeting past,
A testament that love can last.

Beneath the Bark

Whispers dwell in ancient trees,
Stories carried on the breeze.
Roots that delve in earth so deep,
Secrets that the forest keeps.

Cracks and knots in weathered wood,
Speak of life, misunderstood.
Branches reaching for the sky,
Cradle dreams that flutter by.

Sunlight filters, golden streams,
Dancing leaves in nature's dreams.
Beneath the bark, a world alive,
Where the spirits of the forest thrive.

Nature's heart beats strong and true,
Each layer holds a point of view.
In the shade where silence lingers,
Life's symphony plays on fingers.

Nature's Quiet Echo

In the woods where shadows play,
Soft whispers guide the day.
Leaves converse in gentle tones,
Nature hums, and silence moans.

A babbling brook sings clear,
Crickets chirp, so near, so dear.
Each rustle tells a tale,
In the breeze, our souls set sail.

Mountains stand with majesty,
Guardians of the memory.
Sunrise paints the sky in gold,
In each hue, a story told.

Beneath the stars, we find our place,
Nature's echo, a warm embrace.
In quiet moments, hearts align,
As life unfolds, divine, benign.

Mapping the Unseen

In shadows deep, the dreams reside,
A map of hope, where hearts confide.
Each drawn line, a path unknown,
In the silence, seeds are sown.

With every step, the future grows,
A canvas where the mind bestows.
Unwritten stories wait in line,
As stars above begin to shine.

Through tangled thoughts and fleeting fears,
We trace the past, embracing tears.
The compass points to truth and grace,
In every turn, a sacred space.

The unseen guide our every quest,
In whispers soft, we find our rest.
With hearts attuned, we boldly roam,
Mapping dreams, we find our home.

Origins and Journeys

In the cradle of time, we begin,
Footsteps echo where dreams have been.
Whispers of ages, the past holds tight,
As we wander through shadows of light.

Beneath ancient stars, our stories weave,
The threads of fate, in patterns we cleave.
Each path taken, a lesson learned,
In the flames of our hearts, hope is burned.

From mountains high to oceans wide,
We dance through the moments, side by side.
Embrace the unknown, let courage chime,
In every heartbeat, we conquer time.

Winding through valleys, the journey grows,
In every challenge, our spirit flows.
With roots deep-set and dreams in flight,
We touch the horizon, ignite the night.

The Fire Within

A flicker ignites in the depths of the soul,
Burning brightly, it makes us whole.
A flame of passion, fierce and bold,
Tales of our dreams, waiting to be told.

Through storms that rage and shadows that
crawl,
This fire within me will never fall.
It dances and sways, a vibrant call,
With every heartbeat, I rise, not stall.

In moments of doubt, I nourish the spark,
Let it guide me through the smallest of dark.
For within this heart, a volcano erupts,
Creating new worlds, where hope corrupts.

So let the embers glow in the night,
With every challenge, I find my light.
This fire within, forever it stays,
A beacon of strength, igniting my ways.

Whispers of Ancestors

In shadows deep, they softly call,
Their tales entwined, a timeless thrall.
Each whispered word, a gentle breeze,
Awakens roots beneath the trees.

Memories dance on the edge of night,
Faces flicker in soft moonlight.
Silent echoes of ages past,
Stories woven, forever cast.

Through whispered paths where secrets sleep,
Their voices linger, calm and deep.
With every breath, the past ignites,
A tapestry of ancient nights.

So listen close, let their songs flow,
In every heart, their wisdom grows.
Ancestral ties, a sacred thread,
In whispers soft, the lost are fed.

Echoes Beneath the Surface

Beneath the waves, the whispers call,
Secrets hidden, in shadows fall.
Ripples dance, a soft refrain,
Echoes linger, calling again.

In depths of blue, where silence reigns,
Ancient stories flow through veins.
Fish glide by, like thoughts gone stray,
In ocean depths, where dreams drift away.

The tide brings forth the past anew,
Each wave a memory breaking through.
In watery worlds, lost voices sing,
Resounding deep, the truths they bring.

Dive below, where echoes thrive,
In hidden depths, the past survives.
A symphony of life alive,
In the ocean's heart, we all strive.

Grounded in History

In ancient tales, the stones still speak,
Wisdom passed through whispers low.
Echoes linger in shadows deep,
Roots entwined where old winds blow.

Battles fought where we now stand,
Marks of time in every stone.
Footsteps trace the dust of land,
Memories weave a story grown.

Through gilded ages, lessons learned,
Pages yellowed, yet they gleam.
For in the heart, the past is burned,
Guiding us towards a dream.

Bridges built on stories shared,
Threads connect each soul and heart.
In unity, we are prepared,
To honor where the past imparts.

The Spiral of Becoming

In quiet moments, we unfold,
A journey wrapped in time's embrace.
Each twist, a chapter yet untold,
We dance through shadows, find our place.

Growth, a spiral, ever wide,
Lessons learned and bridges built.
In every heart, dreams reside,
The seeds of hope, where love is spilt.

From fragile beginnings, strength is found,
Wounds that heal, our scars create.
In circles drawn upon the ground,
We rise anew, we navigate.

Embrace the ebb, the flow of change,
A canvas drawn with vibrant hues.
Through every step, life feels estranged,
In becoming, we find the muse.

The Understory of Us

In shadows deep, we find our way,
Whispers linger where branches sway.
Roots entwined beneath the ground,
Silent stories yet unbound.

Leaves above, a vibrant hue,
Each color speaks of me and you.
In gentle rustles, secrets greet,
Our hearts echo with love's heartbeat.

Dappled light falls soft and sweet,
In this embrace, we're incomplete.
Yet still we grow, close as we are,
In the understory, we've come far.

With every storm, we bend but stand,
Together here, hand in hand.
In the stillness, whispers trust,
In this world, it's just us.

Beneath the Surface

Beneath the waves, a dance unfolds,
Silent stories, softly told.
Rippling truths in shadows play,
Secrets linger, night and day.

Coral dreams in colors bright,
Life abounds in hidden light.
Silent currents, ebb and flow,
In this place, our spirits grow.

Anemones sway with grace so bold,
In the depths, warmth against the cold.
Amongst the reefs, we drift and glide,
In this world, we must reside.

With every tide, we find our way,
In the depths where shadows play.
Beneath the surface, love does dive,
In this realm, we truly thrive.

Labyrinths of Lore

In shadows deep, the stories weave,
Forgotten tales the echoes leave.
Through winding paths and ancient bricks,
The heart finds solace in the mix.

Each turn a whisper, secrets told,
In every breath, a world unfolds.
The stars above, a guide so bright,
In mysteries, we seek the light.

With quiet steps, we trace the maze,
In twilight's glow, we spend our days.
The threads of fate, so finely spun,
In labyrinths, the journey's fun.

So venture forth, embrace the thrill,
In hidden paths, our spirits fill.
The lore awaits, with open hands,
In winding ways, our story stands.

Reflections in the Silent Forest

Beneath the trees, in muted grace,
The forest holds a sacred space.
With every rustle, whispers play,
In nature's arms, we drift away.

The sunlight dances on the stream,
While shadows weave a gentle dream.
Each leaf a echo, soft and sweet,
In stillness found, our hearts will meet.

The pine trees stand, steadfast and tall,
Guardians of stories, large and small.
In quietude, the mind takes flight,
In the forest's embrace, all feels right.

So linger here, in shadows cast,
Hold tight the moments, let them last.
For in this stillness, truth reveals,
In silent woods, the spirit heals.

The Colors of Our Past

In hues of gold, the memories gleam,
We danced in fields, lost in a dream.
Whispers of laughter, echoes of joy,
Time paints our story, girl and boy.

Shadows and light, they intertwine,
Each brush of fate, a secret sign.
Crimson sunsets, twilight's embrace,
Captured moments, a fleeting grace.

With each bold stroke, the canvas unveils,
Lessons we've learned, and bittersweet tales.
Past's vibrant theme, our hearts decide,
A masterpiece woven, with love as our guide.

Colors dim fade, but never erase,
In every heartbeat, a lingering trace.
The art of remembrance, alive and vast,
In the rich tapestry of our past.

Sunlit Secrets

Golden rays peek through the trees,
Whispers of sunlight dance with the breeze.
In the mornings bright, truths softly unfold,
Stories of life, in whispers retold.

Beneath the stars, secrets confide,
In shadows that linger, where dreams abide.
Nature's embrace, a silent decree,
In the heart's quiet, we find the key.

Petals unfurl in the glow of dawn,
Every soft moment, a new day drawn.
Sunlit whispers, the world slows down,
Each shimmer of light, nature's crown.

In laughter and love, the sun takes flight,
Illuminating all, with pure delight.
Chasing the shadows, our fears disperse,
With sunlit secrets, we find our verse.

The Soul's Tapestry

Threads of gold in the soft light,
Woven tales of dreams and night.
Each color whispers, secrets old,
In patterns bright, a story told.

Beneath the surface, echoes lie,
A silent song, a gentle sigh.
Each stitch a moment, joy or pain,
A tapestry that binds again.

In every knot, a memory stays,
Fading whispers of passing days.
Together they weave, they dance and twine,
The soul's design, an art divine.

Look closely now, the truth revealed,
In this fabric, hearts are healed.
A tapestry of love and grace,
A reflection of the human race.

Forgotten Footprints

Along the shore, the sands shift slow,
Whispers of laughter where memories flow.
Footprints linger, a fleeting trace,
Of moments held in time and space.

The tide will rise, the tide will fall,
Yet still those marks, they speak to all.
Stories hidden in grains so fine,
Forgotten footprints, once divine.

Echoes fade, but love remains,
In every step, joy and pain.
A path once walked, now overgrown,
In silence, the heart has known.

So walk with me, through shadows cast,
Together we'll recall the past.
For every footprint tells a tale,
Of where we've been, where we may sail.

The Ground Beneath

Beneath the grass, the earth does lie,
Whispered secrets, low and shy.
Roots entwined in silent night,
Softly cradling dreams of flight.

Echoes linger in the soil,
Stories woven, time's loyal toil.
With every step, a tale unfolds,
Of ancient paths and hands that hold.

In morning light, the dew does gleam,
Reflecting life, our shared dream.
Each drop a world, a moment's grace,
Life renewing in this sacred space.

The ground beneath, a tapestry spun,
Of all that's lost, and all that's won.
Together we stand, roots intertwined,
With every heartbeat, love defined.

Threads of Connection

In distant lands, we're bound by thread,
Invisible ties, where words are led.
Through laughter shared, through tears we find,
A woven fabric, soft and kind.

Each smile a stitch, each frown a seam,
Crafting a story, a shared dream.
Across the miles, we find our way,
In every night and golden day.

Through trials faced, our colors blend,
A tapestry woven, heart to mend.
Threads of hope in darkest hours,
Strength in numbers, love empowers.

As seasons change, our threads remain,
Binding our hearts through joy and pain.
Together we rise, no need to pretend,
In this vast web, we are friends.

The Lost Tides

In whispers soft, the ocean sighs,
As shadows dance beneath the skies.
The boats drift slow on glassy seas,
Where time forgets, and hearts find ease.

The moon hangs low with silver beams,
It pulls the waves, it stirs our dreams.
But tides once bold now fade away,
Leaving the shores in disarray.

The shells lie scattered, tales untold,
Of tempests fierce and sailors bold.
Yet in the stillness of the night,
The lost tides whisper of their plight.

So cast your nets, embrace the loss,
For every wave must bear its cross.
In every ebb, a story lives,
In every flow, the ocean gives.

Imprints on the Earth

In footprints deep upon the sand,
We carve our dreams, we make our stand.
Each step we take, a mark we leave,
A silent promise to believe.

The forests hum with tales of old,
In every tree, a secret's told.
The rivers run in paths so clear,
Reflecting hopes, dispelling fear.

Mountains rise like giants strong,
Guarding dreams that linger long.
Their peaks reach high, where eagles soar,
While valleys cradle tales of lore.

The earth, it bears our joys and strife,
In every stone, a brush with life.
So let us tread with love and grace,
Creating imprints in this space.

Tides of the Past

Whispers of waves, soft and low,
Carrying tales of long ago.
Footprints washed on golden sand,
Echoes of dreams that slip from hand.

Memories dance as the sun dips low,
Painting the sky with a warm, soft glow.
Time's gentle pull, a constant tide,
Flowing with secrets we cannot hide.

Each crest and trough, a story spun,
Of laughter shared, of battles won.
Beneath the surface, currents swirl,
Holding our past in an endless whirl.

Yet as the moon calls the sea to play,
We learn to embrace the coming day.
For the tides of the past, though vast and deep,
Guide us forward, as we dare to leap.

Shadows of the Forgotten

In the corners where darkness lingers,
Whispers of past slip through fingers.
Faint echoes call from weary walls,
Casting their spell as night softly falls.

Once filled with laughter, now silent and still,
Time drapes its cloak with an unspoken will.
Memories drift in the hush of the night,
Lost tales entwined in the fading light.

Ghosts of the old dance in twilight's embrace,
Glances of joy in a worn-out space.
Though shadows may creep, and the light may
wane,
The heart remembers, and love will remain.

In the depths of silence, stories reside,
Of those we cherish, of whom we've cried.
Embrace the shadows, for they are a part,
Of the journey we share, of the depth of the

heart.

Patterns of Existence

In shadows cast, we find our way,
Through winding paths of night and day.
Each choice we make, a thread we weave,
In patterns wrought, we learn to believe.

Mountains rise and rivers flow,
Life's cycle turns, forever we grow.
In silence speaks the heart's old song,
We dance in the realms where we belong.

With every breath, the moments blend,
Connections form, on love we depend.
Like stars that flicker in the vast night,
In patterns bright, we seek the light.

In the end, we all return,
To lessons learned, to fires that burn.
In the tapestry, our stories blend,
Patterns of existence, love without end.

The Well of Remembrance

Down in the depths, where shadows dwell,
Lies the ancient, silent well.
Whispers echo, tales untold,
In water deep, our dreams unfold.

Memories rise like bubbles in air,
Fleeting glimpses, moments rare.
Each drop reflects a face or place,
A tender touch, a warm embrace.

When weary hearts seek solace still,
They gather near the wishing well.
With every thought, a ripple sways,
In the depths of time, love forever stays.

So cast your wishes, let them flow,
Into the well where sweet truths grow.
For in remembrance, we find our past,
Eternal echoes that ever last.

Shadows of Our Forebears

In the twilight of the past, they stand,
Figures etched in forgotten sand.
Whispers of wisdom in the breeze,
Carried on thc rustling leaves.

Footsteps echo on ancient trails,
Stories woven in wind and gales.
Their laughter dances in the air,
A legacy we all must share.

Ghostly smiles in faded light,
Guiding us through the night.
With every choice, their shadows guide,
In their memory, we abide.

Each dawn reveals their silent grace,
In our hearts, they find a place.
Shadows whisper, time stands still,
In every heartbeat, we feel their will.

Mirrors of Identity

In the glass, reflections show,
A tapestry of joys and woes.
Fragments of self, pieced together,
A mosaic shaped by time and weather.

Voices blend, cultures meet,
In every heart, a rhythmic beat.
Threads of past, future's thread,
In this mirror, truth is spread.

Faces change, but spirits stay,
Guiding us along the way.
Here we find our common ground,
In diverse stories, love is found.

Each glance reveals a deeper tale,
Through storms and calm, we set our sail.
Mirrors echo what we share,
Unity found in every stare.

A Journey to the Center

Through winding paths, we make our way,
In quest of whispers, lost in sway.
Beneath the earth, secrets lie,
Calling softly, asking why.

With each step, the world dims down,
Ancient echoes in timeless crown.
Shadows dance in cavern's glow,
Revealing tales we long to know.

The heart of silence beats so strong,
In this embrace, we feel we belong.
A spiral journey, deep within,
Where life begins and dreams begin.

Emerging back, our souls have changed,
From depths of earth, we are re-arranged.
With eyes opened, we take our flight,
To share our truth, into the light.

The Buried Stories

Underneath the soil so rich,
Lies a history, an ancient stitch.
Whispers of lives, both brave and bold,
In every grain, a tale unfolds.

Forgotten dreams beneath our feet,
Echoes of laughter, sorrow's beat.
Every rock, a witness stands,
To love's embrace and parting hands.

Veins of the earth hold stories tight,
In the darkness, they seek the light.
From roots and bones, the past remains,
In every storm, in every rain.

Digging deep, we find our past,
Connecting threads that ever last.
With every story, we are reborn,
In the tapestry of night and dawn.

Serpentines of Memory

In shadows deep where whispers dwell,
Fragments of dreams weave a spell.
Each twist and turn, a story unfolds,
In the heart's embrace, secrets hold.

Echoes dance on the edge of night,
Fleeting moments, lost in flight.
Memories coil like smoke in air,
Fading softly, rare and fair.

Time's river flows, both swift and slow,
Beneath the surface, currents glow.
Serpentines trace what once was clear,
Leaving shadows, drawing near.

Yet in the maze of what we've known,
Buds of wisdom softly grown.
For every turn, a lesson to gain,
In serpentines, we break the chain.

Silent Currents

Beneath the surface, secrets glide,
Silent currents, deep and wide.
Carrying whispers of the past,
In their flow, memories cast.

Ripples shimmer on tranquil waves,
Tales of longing that the silence saves.
Every heartbeat in the stream,
An echo of a distant dream.

Shadows flicker in twilight's grace,
Time drifts by, a hushed embrace.
Silent currents, softly sway,
Guiding thoughts that drift away.

In the depth, a truth resides,
Awakened dreams where silence hides.
In gentle flows, we find our way,
Through silent currents, come what may.

Visions of the Subconscious

In the quiet of the night, dreams unfurl,
Whispers of the heart, a secret swirl.
Shadows dance lightly on the edge of thought,
Threads of hidden truths, delicatcly caught.

Images flicker, like stars in the sky,
Each one a memory, a reason to fly.
Voices that beckon from deep within,
A labyrinth of feelings, where fears begin.

Colors blend softly, a canvas alive,
Here in this realm, imagination can thrive.
Waves of emotion ripple through calm seas,
Unlocking the door with a gentle breeze.

Fragments of stories weave in and out,
A tapestry rich, a dance of doubt.
The subconscious whispers, a powerful guide,
In the heart's hidden chambers, we must confide.

The Pulse of the Earth

Beneath our feet, the heartbeat resonates,
A rhythm of life, where all creation waits.
Mountains rise high, valleys softly sway,
Nature's song sings, both night and day.

Rivers flow gently, carving their path,
Echoes of history in each gentle bath.
From deserts so vast to oceans so wide,
The pulse of the Earth, a boundless tide.

Whispers of wind through the leaves do glide,
Tales of the ancients in each turning tide.
The silence speaks volumes, a wisdom so grand,
In every grain of sand, a story does stand.

With every dawn's light, shadows retreat,
The heartbeat grows strong, the world wakes on
feet.
Feel the connection, the bond that we share,
In the pulse of the Earth, we find our prayer.

Reverberations of the Heart

In whispers soft, the echoes call,
A heartbeat's rhythm, gentle thrall.
Through shadows deep, the secrets weave,
A tapestry of love, we believe.

With every pulse, a story spun,
Through laughter shared and tears we run.
The silent murmurs, the joy, the pain,
In every moment, love remains.

A glance exchanged, a silent plea,
In every breath, you're here with me.
The world may shift, but we will stand,
Together united, hand in hand.

As stars align in the midnight sky,
Our hearts collide, as time slips by.
Resonating dreams, we dare to chase,
In reverberations, we find our place.

Traces of Timelessness

In the stillness of a whispered night,
Memories linger, soft and bright.
Each moment stirs like gentle waves,
Carving paths in the heart that saves.

The echoes hum of ages past,
In fleeting seconds, shadows cast.
With every breath, a story grows,
Through timeless depths, love ever flows.

A dance of stars in endless flight,
Threads of fate weave day and night.
In every glance, eternity found,
In fleeting joy, we're tightly bound.

Past and present, intertwined tight,
In traces of timelessness, we ignite.
Bound by the moments we hold so dear,
In the fabric of time, love draws near.

Mapping Internal Landscapes

In the quiet corners, shadows play,
Thoughts weave through, night and day,
Memories bloom like wildflowers,
Crafting maps in reflection's hours.

Faint echoes whisper, lost in time,
Winding paths in rhythm and rhyme,
Journeys charted beneath the skin,
Awakening stories harbored within.

Hills of sorrow, valleys of joy,
Each landscape shaped, none can destroy,
Journey onward, unveil the maze,
In hearts reside countless ways.

As twilight drapes its gentle shawl,
I wander forth, heeding the call,
Every turn a chance to explore,
Mapping landscapes forevermore.

Silhouettes of Legacy

In the dusk of dreams, shadows rise,
Echoes linger, weaving ties,
Legacy held in fragile hands,
Silhouettes dance on shifting sands.

Whispers from those who came before,
Stories etched on memory's floor,
Guiding lights, they softly gleam,
A tapestry spun from a timeless dream.

Roots entwined in sacred ground,
In every heartbeat, their love is found,
Embers glow in the night's embrace,
Footprints marked in this shared space.

Carry forth their hopes and fears,
Through laughter, joy, and silent tears,
Silhouettes linger, forever stay,
In our hearts, they lead the way.

When Histories Collide

In shadows where the past does dwell,
Echoes of voices, stories to tell.
Time weaves its threads, a tapestry grand,
Where destinies meet, and ages stand.

Moments collide, a dance so strange,
Fates intertwine, in paths that change.
Silent whispers of what could have been,
In the intersection of loss and win.

Fragments of time in a fractured glass,
Reflecting the dreams of those who pass.
Each scar a reminder of battles fought,
In the silent spaces where histories are sought.

Yet in the chaos, a beauty unfolds,
Stories of courage, and warmth to behold.
Through the clashing we find our way,
In the light of the dawn, a brand new day.

Hidden Valleys of Thought

Beneath the surface, where ideas creep,
In hidden valleys, our secrets sleep.
Whispers of wisdom in silence bloom,
Nature's own canvas, a quiet room.

Dreams take root in the fertile ground,
In shadows of doubt, new truths are found.
Winding paths through the forests of mind,
Each twist and turn leaves old fears behind.

Rivers of thought flow deep and wide,
Carving through rocks where answers hide.
In the stillness, a spark ignites,
Guiding us gently through starry nights.

With each sunrise, new light reveals,
The hidden valleys where knowledge heals.
In the embrace of the quiet night,
We find our way, towards the light.

The Depths Beneath Us

In shadows deep where secrets dwell,
A whisper stirs, a hidden spell.
The echoes call from ancient stone,
In silence held, the past is grown.

Beneath the waves, where darkness reigns,
A world of dreams and subtle chains.
The currents pull, a silent plea,
To seek the heart of mystery.

Roots intertwine through earth and time,
A pulse beneath the surface rhyme.
Beneath the weight of all we see,
A depth alive with history.

The journey calls, we must descend,
To find the truth that seems to bend.
With open hearts, we delve and dive,
In depths unknown, the soul's alive.

Unfolding Inner Landscapes

In quiet moments, thoughts take flight,
A canvas bare, a spark ignites.
Colors swirl in vivid hues,
Each brushstroke speaks of hidden views.

Through valleys deep, and mountains high,
The spirit roams, the heart does fly.
A journey drawn by dreams untold,
In every breath, a story bold.

With every step, the paths reveal,
The layers soft, the truths we feel.
In gardens wild, where shadows play,
We find the light, we chase the day.

As petals fold and blossoms bloom,
The inner world dispels the gloom.
With open eyes and hearts set free,
We wander through our tapestry.

Seeds of Yesterday

In the soil where memories lay,
Whispers of dreams softly sway.
Roots entwined in stories old,
Glimmers of truth in tales retold.

Time has woven a tapestry bright,
Each thread a glimpse of the past's light.
With every bloom, a lesson grows,
In the heart where affection flows.

Beneath the sun's warming grace,
Seeds of hope find their place.
With rain, they soak and expand,
Carrying dreams across the land.

When autumn winds begin to sigh,
Leaves will dance, and seasons fly.
Yet in the chill of winter's hold,
The seeds lie waiting, brave and bold.

The Hidden Flow

Beneath the surface, a current runs,
Silent whispers, the language of suns.
In shadows where secrets dwell,
The river of life spins its spell.

Ripples of thoughts in the night air,
Echoes of dreams, a delicate snare.
With every pulse, a story brews,
Of hopes and heartaches, the unseen dues.

In the silence, a symphony plays,
In the depths where the heart obeys.
Drifting gently through time and space,
The hidden flow finds its grace.

Waves of change wash ashore,
Carrying whispers of what's in store.
Through the stillness, we come to know,
The richness of life in the hidden flow.

Echoes of Existence

Upon the shadowed hill, we stand,
Whispers of time slip through our hands.
Memories linger, soft like dew,
In echoes of existence, old yet new.

Life's fleeting breath, a gentle sigh,
Moments captured, as the world goes by.
In the quiet night, stars align,
Reminding us of what is divine.

Yet in this dance of light and shade,
The paths we tread, the choices made.
Every heartbeat, a story spun,
In echoes of existence, we are one.

Let the dawn break, unveil the truth,
In the laughter and tears of vibrant youth.
With every dawn, we rise and fall,
Echoes of existence, we recall.

Navigating the Forgotten

In the corners of dreams where shadows play,
Forgotten tales whisper, lost in the fray.
We search for the light, amidst the dark,
Navigating the forgotten, we leave our mark.

Silent paths hold secrets deep,
In the folds of time, memories sleep.
With every step, the past ignites,
Guiding us gently towards new heights.

The echoes of voices, soft and low,
Lead us through places we long to know.
Each turn reveals a hidden song,
Navigating the forgotten, we belong.

Through twisted trails and overgrown lanes,
The heartbeat of history remains.
With hearts as compasses, we find our way,
Navigating the forgotten, come what may.

The Heart of the Earth

Beneath the roots, where shadows creep,
The whispers of the soil deep.
Life pulses gently, rich and bold,
In the heart of Earth, stories unfold.

Mountains rise, with secrets shared,
In every stone, a memory bared.
Rivers flow, like threads of fate,
Weaving tales to resonate.

The winds carry songs of the past,
In the quiet, echoes cast.
Flora blooms in vibrant hues,
In the heart of Earth, the muse imbues.

Listen close, and you will find,
Nature sings, both soft and kind.
For in each breath, in every gleam,
Lies the heart of Earth's eternal dream.

Time's Silhouette

Shadows dance on the wall's embrace,
Moments captured, a fleeting trace.
The clock ticks softly, a subtle guide,
In time's silhouette, we must abide.

Memories swirl, like autumn leaves,
Whispers of ages, the heart believes.
Each second blooms, then fades away,
In time's embrace, we learn to sway.

Days blend into a canvas bright,
Painting dreams in the soft twilight.
Time marches on, a steady flow,
In its silhouette, we learn to grow.

Glimpses of future, shadows of past,
In every heartbeat, moments cast.
Hold them dearly, let them spin,
For time's silhouette draws us in.

Liminal Spaces of Self

In shadows cast by twilight's glow,
I wander paths where echoes flow.
A tender truth, a silent plea,
In every step, I seek to be.

Fragments of dreams in starlit skies,
Yet in between, a quiet rise.
The space between the known and new,
A whispered voice that leads me through.

Faces change like drifting sands,
Waves of time slip through my hands.
I find my place in shifting hues,
A canvas vast, a heart imbues.

In liminal breaths, the self unfolds,
With every heartbeat, truth beholds.
Embracing all that lies in wait,
The dance of self, a shifting fate.

Forgotten Roots of Identity

Beneath the soil, old stories sleep,
Whispers of roots buried deep.
In tangled thorns and twisted vines,
Lie echoes of forgotten signs.

Branches reaching, yearning high,
Connecting with the endless sky.
Yet in the dark, the past resides,
In every shadow, truth abides.

In mirrors cracked, reflections fade,
Memories lost in time's parade.
A journey stitched with threads of pain,
Through fleeting joy, I search again.

From scattered seeds, new blooms arise,
Each petal holds where silence lies.
The roots will whisper, though so far,
My identity, an ancient star.

Currents of Memory

Whispers of the past entwine,
In shadows cast by fleeting light,
Each moment caught, a sacred sign,
Drifts softly through the endless night.

Familiar faces blend and fade,
Their laughter echoes in my mind,
A tapestry of joy once laid,
Now threads of longing intertwined.

Fragments dance upon the breeze,
Like leaves that twirl in autumn's grace,
Reminders held in gentle ease,
Each heartbeat finds a sacred space.

Waves of nostalgia rise and fall,
A river winding through my soul,
With every memory, I recall,
The depth of love that makes me whole.

The Fabric of Time

Stitch by stitch, the moments grow,
Woven tight in golden thread,
Each instance, like a river's flow,
A path where dreams and thoughts are wed.

Colors blend in hues so bright,
Dancing patterns in twilight's glow,
Time unfurls its endless flight,
A canvas where our hopes do flow.

Silent echoes, soft and clear,
In every fold, a story lives,
Layers crafted year by year,
The gift of time, a heart that gives.

As the needle passes through,
We shape our fate, a choice defined,
In woven patterns, old and new,
The fabric of our lives aligned.

Veins of the Earth

Beneath the soil, secrets lie,
Roots entwined, whispering shy.
Life pulses through each hidden way,
Veins of the earth, in night and day.

Mountains rise, ancient and wise,
Cradling tales beneath the skies.
In every stone, a story beams,
Echoing soft like distant dreams.

Rivers flow, a silver thread,
Carving paths where few dare tread.
Every drop, a memory clear,
A dance of life that draws us near.

From deep below to heights above,
The earth unveils its endless love.
In every heartbeat, every breath,
We find the pulse, the dance of death.

Threads of the Unseen

In shadows cast, the whispers weave,
Tales of magic, bold and naïve.
Threads of fate in twilight spun,
Binding hearts till day is done.

The moonlight glows on secrets kept,
In silent corners where dreams are leapt.
An unseen touch, a brush so light,
Guides the wanderers through the night.

Eyes meet softly, a spark ignites,
Two souls entwined in silent flights.
The fabric of the world, unseen,
Holds all the moments we've between.

Through the tapestry, colors blend,
Life's an art we must defend.
Each thread connects, a fragile zone,
In this vast web, we are not alone.

Echos of the Untold

Whispers linger in the night,
Stories hidden from the light.
Voices soft, yet crystal clear,
Carrying tales we long to hear.

In shadows deep, where secrets lie,
Hopeful dreams begin to sigh.
Footsteps echo on the ground,
In silence, truth can often be found.

Time is a river, flowing slow,
Worn-out paths, where none dare go.
Each heart holds a tale to tell,
Echos rising from the well.

Listen close, the world confesses,
Through the dark, it gently presses.
In every corner, every fold,
Lives a story never told.

Beneath the Canopy

Leaves are dancing in the breeze,
Whispers rustle through the trees.
Sunlight filters, warm and bright,
Nature's stage, a pure delight.

Mossy beds and hidden trails,
Where the song of silence pales.
Creatures peep through branches green,
Life unfolds in every scene.

Stars peek through the leafy dome,
In this space, we find our home.
Shadows stretch and gently sway,
Guiding us through night and day.

Beneath the canopy's embrace,
Nature wears a timeless grace.
In this world, both calm and free,
We discover who we can be.

The Foundation of Us

In whispers soft, our dreams align,
Brick by brick, we build a sign.
Trust and love, the mortar mix,
Through storms we'll stand, through shadows
fix.

With hands held tight, we face the night,
In laughter shared, we'll find our light.
Roots entwined, like ancient trees,
Together bound by destiny's breeze.

Each tale we weave, a thread so fine,
In everyday moments, your hand in mine.
Life's tapestry rich, yet simple too,
The foundation strong, built just for you.

So here's to us, through thick and thin,
Together forever, where love begins.
A masterpiece forged, just as we trust,
In the journey of life, it's the foundation of us.

Constellations of the Past

Stars of yore, in the night they glow,
Tales of life, in whispers flow.
Each spark a memory, lost but clear,
Guiding dreams, like a wink from near.

In shadows cast, through time we roam,
Mapping paths that lead us home.
Echoes linger, in softest sighs,
Reflecting moments beneath deep skies.

A canvas drawn with light and grace,
The constellations, our sacred space.
In silence shared, we find our way,
Tracing wonders from yesterday.

So let us gaze, and breathe the night,
In dreamy realms, we'll take our flight.
Each star a story, twinkling vast,
Connecting hearts with constellations of the
past.

Harvesting the Past

In fields of gold, where memories grow,
We gather whispers of long ago.
The sunlit days held laughter loud,
Among the roots, the silence plowed.

With hands of time, we sift the grain,
Each kernel holds a trace of pain.
The harvest song, a bittersweet tune,
Echoes softly beneath the moon.

The seasons change, as seasons do,
Yet in our hearts, the old stays true.
We plant our seeds in fertile ground,
In past's embrace, our hope is found.

So let us gather, let us weave,
The threads of past, what we believe.
For in this tapestry we find,
The echo of a life designed.

The Terrain of Thought

In valleys deep where shadows creep,
Ideas rise like mountains steep.
A winding path through fog and light,
The mind's vast realm, both day and night.

Each thought a seed, each dream a tree,
Rooted strong in mystery.
The rivers flow with currents bright,
Carving canyons, shaping sight.

Amidst the peaks, the quiet breath,
A sacred space, outlasting death.
Exploring realms beyond the grey,
Curiosity lights the way.

Navigating storms that brew,
In every thought, a view anew.
So trek the landscape of your mind,
For wisdom waits, just seek and find.

The Hidden Chronicles

In shadows deep where secrets dwell,
Whispers float like a hidden bell.
Moments lost in time's embrace,
Forgotten tales, a ghostly trace.

Pages worn by hands of fate,
Stories linger, though they wait.
A flicker of truth, a hint of light,
In the silence, echoes ignite.

Voices call from distant shores,
Unlock the past, open the doors.
Each memory, a thread to weave,
In the fabric of dreams we believe.

Beneath the stars, the past runs free,
A tapestry of what used to be.
Listen closely, embark on the quest,
For hidden chronicles are truly blessed.

Seeds of Remembrance

In the garden where memories bloom,
Seeds of remembrance dispel the gloom.
Each petal unfurls a story untold,
Whispers of love, both young and old.

Roots intertwined, they stand so tall,
Carrying echoes that gently call.
With every breeze, a sigh descends,
For the moments cherished, the heart defends.

Time may fade, but hope remains,
In every drop of falling rains.
Nurtured dreams beneath the ground,
In the silence, their voice resounds.

So plant your heart in fertile earth,
Let nostalgia thrive, give it worth.
For seeds of today can bloom anew,
In gardens where memories still shine through.

Wilderness of the Mind

In the depths of thoughts, shadows play,
Where whispers echo, lost in the sway.
Paths overgrown, tangled in time,
A labyrinth of dreams, an untamed rhyme.

Winds of memory, cold and warm,
Shaping the silence, a quiet storm.
Each corner turned, a story unfolds,
In the wilderness of the mind, truth holds.

Echoes of laughter, traces of tears,
Woven together through all the years.
In the wilderness vast, where visions blend,
I wander alone, yet never alone, my friend.

Through valleys of doubt and peaks of bliss,
In every heartbeat, a moment we miss.
The mind's wild expanse, a journey unkind,
Forever exploring the wilderness of the mind.

Ripples of the Ancestors

In the quiet dusk, whispers arise,
Stories of old, beneath the skies.
Ripples of wisdom, woven so tight,
Guiding our souls through the dark and the light.

The echoes of footsteps, long gone yet near,
Each tale a reminder, a song we hear.
In the leaves of the forest, in rivers that flow,
Ancestors wait, their love still aglow.

Through the storms of time, resilience thrives,
In the fabric of kin, the essence survives.
Ripples of courage, lifelines we trace,
Holding our spirits in an ancient embrace.

With each gentle nudge, we honor their fight,
Carrying forth, their dreams in our sight.
Ripples of the past, in our hearts they blend,
An eternal bond, with the love of our ancestors

we mend.

Beneath the Canopy

The leaves above whisper tales,
In the dance of the gentle breeze.
Sunlight filters through the trails,
Casting shadows with graceful ease.

Roots intertwine deep in the earth,
Holding stories of growth and strife.
Beneath the green, there's a rebirth,
A sacred place cradling life.

Whispers of ancient trees call,
To wanderers seeking their way.
Each step echoes a timeless thrall,
As nature invites them to stay.

For in this realm, secrets abide,
In the rustle, the hush, the song.
Beneath the canopy's wide tide,
Hearts and souls finally belong.

Truths Entwined

In the shadows where whispers dwell,
Two hearts beat in synchronized time.
Secrets shared in a silent spell,
Truths entwined in a melodious rhymc.

Promises held in a tender gaze,
Unraveling stories of hope and fear.
Through life's long and winding maze,
These truths keep the path ever clear.

With every storm that may arise,
Their bond grows stronger with each strife.
Together they soar through the skies,
Finding solace in shared life.

In the tapestry woven of fate,
Threads of love brightly shine.
In every moment, they create,
A beautiful tale of the divine.

Echoes of the Ancients

In shadows deep, they softly speak,
The tales of time, both strong and weak.
Lost songs of ages, weaving through,
Their wisdom waits for hearts that view.

From cliffs and stones, the winds arise,
A chorus found beneath the skies.
Each rustling leaf, each whispering breath,
Holds secrets of both life and death.

The earth remembers, beats like a drum,
In silent nights, the ancients hum.
Their stories carved in mountain seams,
Eternal echoes, woven dreams.

So listen close, let silence be,
The link to those who roamed so free.
In every shadow, hear the call,
Of echoes rising, never fall.

Whispers Beneath the Surface

Beneath the waves, the world holds sway,
In murky depths, the stillness lay.
A gentle pulse, a heartbeat's song,
Where secrets dance, and shadows long.

The water stirs, a silent plea,
For souls to hear, for hearts to see.
In tides that pull, in currents swift,
There lies a magic, a sacred gift.

Rise up from depths, the softest sigh,
A language formed, as time drifts by.
With every ripple, a story blends,
Of ancient realms where silence transcends.

So dive within, embrace the flow,
In whispers lost, a world to know.
The surface gleams, a mirror bright,
Reflecting dreams in the hush of night.

Memories In Bloom

In gardens rich with fragrant light,
Soft whispers float, a sweet delight.
Where petals dance on gentle breeze,
Past echoes hum beneath the trees.

A childhood's laugh, a fleeting glance,
Each moment held in timeless trance.
With every bloom, a tale retold,
Of joy and dreams in colors bold.

The sun dips low, the sky ablaze,
In twilight's glow, we drift in haze.
Collecting memories, like dew,
In every petal, love shines through.

As seasons change, so too our hearts,
Yet in this garden, beauty starts.
In bloom, the past and present meet,
A fragrant bond, forever sweet.

Among the Twisted Vines

In shadows deep, the twilight sighs,
Among the vines, where mystery lies.
A labyrinth of green and brown,
Where secrets weave, and dreams are grown.

The tendrils twist like whispered dreams,
Beneath the moon's soft silver beams.
In tangled paths, we find our way,
Through whispered thoughts that softly sway.

With every turn, a story waits,
Of lovers lost and twisted fates.
Among the leaves, their laughter fades,
In echoes deep, where light cascades.

Yet hope remains in every vine,
A promise held, a love divine.
In nature's hold, we'll roam awhile,
Among the twisted vines, we smile.

The Silted Pathways

Worn and twisted, paths unfold,
Beneath the weight of stories told.
Whispers linger in the air,
Each step unearths a silent care.

Nature weaves a gentle shroud,
Amongst the tangled roots endowed.
Time meanders, slow and still,
In shadows deep, the heart can fill.

Mossy carpets greet our feet,
Where sunlight dances, soft and sweet.
Echoes of a distant past,
In every corner, memories cast.

The journey stirs the spirit's quest,
On silted paths, the soul finds rest.
Each bend reveals a new embrace,
In nature's arms, we find our place.

Hidden Canopies

Beneath the boughs, a world concealed,
Where sunlight peeks, secrets revealed.
Leaves whisper tales in rustling tones,
A sanctuary where the heart roams.

Threads of green weave through the air,
Guardians of peace, beyond compare.
Fluttering wings and shadows play,
In hidden canopies, dreams sway.

Streams babble soft, a gentle song,
In nature's fold, we all belong.
A tapestry of life unfolds,
In emerald depths, the purest gold.

Wandering through this whispered glade,
A quiet refuge that won't fade.
In the embrace of branches wide,
True solace blooms, forever abides.

Nourished by Heritage

Roots run deep in the soil,
Stories whispered, a sacred toil.
Traditions dance in the air,
Binding hearts with love and care.

Colors vibrant, threads we weave,
In every pattern, we believe.
Lessons taught by those before,
A legacy we can't ignore.

Nature's bounty, a gift bestowed,
In family gatherings, laughter flowed.
Meals prepared with age-old grace,
Each bite a journey, every taste a trace.

Nourished souls with every meal,
A story shared, a bond we feel.
Heritage wraps like a warm embrace,
In our hearts, we find our place.

The Unseen Past

Whispers of time, gentle and light,
Echoes of voices in the night.
Secrets hidden in the breeze,
Memories dance among the trees.

Footsteps linger on ancient stone,
History etched, never alone.
Shadows of ancients walk with pride,
In the silence, they confide.

Pages worn, tales unspooled,
Legends that time has gently ruled.
In every crack, a story lies,
In every glance, the past defies.

The unseen past, a guiding light,
Through the darkness, it takes flight.
With every heartbeat, we recall,
The threads of history bind us all.

Insights from the Underground

Roots burrow deep through earthy shrouds,
Whispers of wisdom in silence loud.
Beneath the surface, truths reside,
In darkness, light begins to bide.

Glimmers of hope in shadowed lands,
The pulse of life in ancient strands.
Each twist and turn, a journey forged,
In humble depths, the soul is gorged.

Vines climb high, reaching for the sun,
Yet cherish the dark, where it's begun.
For in the underground, stories weave,
Of struggle and strength, we must believe.

The unseen world, a lasting guide,
In the quiet depths, we shall abide.
Embrace the shadows, learn from the past,
Insights from the underground are vast.

Cultivating the Inner World

In the garden of thought, seeds take root,
Nurtured by dreams, in silence, they shoot.
Whispers of growth in the soil of the mind,
Fostering peace, the rarest kind.

Tenderly tending to what lies within,
Pulling up weeds of doubt and sin.
Patience is key as seasons change,
Within our hearts, we re-arrange.

Petals of insight unfold with grace,
Inviting the light to illuminate space.
A symphony blooms, vibrant and bright,
Cultivating calm amid the night.

In reflection's mirror, we come to know,
Harvesting wisdom, watch it grow.
The inner world thrives, nourished by love,
A sacred garden, blessed from above.

Lullabies of the Land

Whispers of the evening breeze,
Softly cradling ancient trees,
Moonlight dances on the ground,
Nature's lullaby, profound.

Stars peek out from velvet skies,
Crickets sing their sweet goodbyes,
Rivers hum a gentle tune,
Underneath the watchful moon.

Fields of dreams in silence lie,
As the night begins to sigh,
Every shadow tells a tale,
Of the night that will prevail.

In this stillness, hearts can mend,
Lullabies that never end,
Holding close the warmth of night,
Till the dawn brings back the light.

Tapestry of Time

Threads of moments weave the past,
Stitched together, memories cast,
Every hue a story told,
In the fabric, love unfolds.

Seasons change with graceful sway,
Colors fade, then bright array,
Time, the weaver, deft and bold,
Spins the yarn of dreams retold.

Whispers echo through the years,
Laughter mingled with our tears,
Each stitch holds a heartbeat's grace,
Life's embrace, a sacred space.

As the threads begin to blend,
A tapestry that has no end,
In every line, our souls align,
Carved in time, forever shine.

Unearthing the Forgotten

In shadows deep where secrets lie,
Old stories whisper, forgotten sigh.
Dusty tomes on wooden shelves,
Echoes of lives, they used to dwell.

Through crumbling walls, the past will show,
Fragments of dreams, a gentle flow.
Images faint, yet spirits glow,
Awakening truths from long ago.

Each brick and stone, a tale unfolds,
Silent witness to broken molds.
Time, the thief, but not eraser,
Unveils the heart of every spacer.

Explore the dark where shadows roam,
Unearth the tales that feel like home.
The forgotten, they yearn to speak,
Their timeless echoes strong, not weak.

A Song of the Unheard

In crowded rooms where silence dwells,
Voices lost in tangled spells.
Hopes and dreams get swept away,
Yearning hearts have much to say.

Soft whispers blend with distant cries,
Echoes linger, beneath the skies.
Each note a plea, each breath a sigh,
A symphony of souls who try.

In shadows cast by blinding light,
Sparks of truth arise from night.
The unheard song will rise once more,
Breaking chains from every shore.

Listen closely, heed the call,
Each story matters, big and small.
Together we can make it heard,
A chorus strong, let voices stir.

Threads of Time

In the fabric of days, we weave our dreams,
Moments stitched tight, or unraveling seams.
Waves of the past wash over our feet,
Each tide a reminder, both bitter and sweet.

Shadows dance lightly on paths we have crossed,

Echoes of laughter, the lines of the lost.
With every tick tock, a story unfolds,
Of love and of loss, of the young and the old.

Time whispers secrets in soft, gentle tones,
Binding our hearts with invisible stones.
Yet in every thread, a hope does reside,
As we journey onward, with stars as our guide.

So cherish the moments, both fleeting and rife,
For each thread of time is a tapestry of life.

Reflections in Still Water

Beneath the calm surface, the world stands still,
Mirrors of dreams and shadows fulfill.
The sky stretches wide, a canvas of blue,
Each ripple a secret, each wave a view.

Leaves gently flutter, kissed by the breeze,
Whispers of nature, the soul's gentle ease.
In the depths of the pond, all worries dissolve,
A moment of peace where the heart can evolve.

Footsteps grow quiet, a pause in the day,
Reflections of life in the soft, warming sway.
Each glance at the water reveals what's inside,
A dance of the spirit, a calm, tranquil guide.

So lean to the surface, let thoughts drift away,
In reflections of stillness, find hope's gentle ray.

The Depths of Yesterday

In whispers of the past we tread,
Memories like shadows dance ahead.
The echoes of laughter, the tears once shed,
Carved in the silence, where dreams are bred.

Each moment a ripple in time's vast sea,
A treasure chest of what used to be.
Lost in the mirror, reflections decree,
The depth of yesterday calls out to me.

Faded photographs, a story untold,
In sepia tones, the warmth of the old.
Each glance a reminder, a heart turned cold,
Yet in the depths, we find courage bold.

So let us wander through time's faded lanes,
Reclaim the beauty amid the pains.
For in every memory, life's essence remains,
The depths of yesterday, where love sustains.

Unraveling Origins

In the cradle of time, a thread we weave,
Tracing the lineage that we believe.
In whispers of ancients, the tales conceive,
Unraveling origins, we dare to perceive.

Through branches of family, roots intertwine,
Secrets held tightly, in shadows they shine.
Each story a bead on a string so fine,
In the web of existence, our fates align.

Paths of our fathers, the steps they took,
In the margins of history, within each book.
The choices, the struggles, the time that it took,
We gather the pieces, our past we unhook.

With every discovery, we breathe, we grow,
Unraveling questions that long lay below.
The tapestry of life, a radiant show,
In unraveling origins, our spirits glow.

Conversations with the Past

Whispers echo in the night,
Memories dance in soft, pale light.
Each shadow tells a tale anew,
Of laughter lost and skies so blue.

Old photographs in faded hues,
Tell stories hidden, seldom used.
Time's gentle hand now holds them tight,
As dreams intertwine with the moon's white
light.

Footsteps linger on dusty floors,
In quiet rooms where love restores.
Fragments of time, like leaves in fall,
Speak secrets in their silent call.

Yet forward I must boldly tread,
With echoes of the past, I'm led.
In every choice, the past does weave,
A tapestry I won't believe.

Branches of Being

Roots dig deep in the earth's embrace,
Branches reach for a boundless space.
Leaves whisper tales of wind and sun,
In every heart, a journey begun.

Nature's canvas, vibrant, alive,
With colors that pulse and thrive.
Each petal holds a sacred song,
Of all that's right and all that's wrong.

Beneath the surface, life abounds,
In hidden corners, joy resounds.
The cycle spins, a dance of fate,
Each moment born, each moment great.

Through storms and calm, together we sway,
Branches of being guide the way.
In unity, we stand so tall,
Together we rise, together we fall.

Grit and Grace

In shadows deep, we stand so tall,
With hearts of steel, we won't yet fall.
Through storms that rage, we find our way,
With grit and grace, we'll face the day.

The mountain high, the valley low,
With every step, our courage grows.
In darkest night, we spark the light,
With grit and grace, we'll win the fight.

The road is long, the path is rough,
But in our hearts, we know we're tough.
We rise again, no time for doubt,
With grit and grace, we'll find our route.

Through trials faced, we mend and heal,
With every scar, our strength reveals.
Together bound, we shall embrace,
The journey worn, with grit and grace.

Treasures from the Past

In ancient halls, where whispers dwell,
Stories linger, weaves a spell.
From dusty tomes to faded maps,
Treasures of old in timeless laps.

The laughter shared, the tears once shed,
Echoes of voices, long since dead.
Fragments of dreams, like stars so bright,
Treasures from past, they guide our light.

In every scar, a lesson hides,
In every turn, the truth abides.
The roots we've grown, in soil so deep,
Treasures from the past, our hearts will keep.

With every tale, a bridge we find,
To worlds of old, where hearts aligned.
We honor those who paved the way,
Treasures from the past, here we stay.

Structures of Belonging

In quiet corners, laughter flows,
Where heartbeats find their rhythm close.
Walls of warmth, built from shared dreams,
Together we weave, or so it seems.

Beneath the stars, our stories blend,
Every whisper, a thread we send.
Roots entwined, in soil we trust,
In golden moments, rise from dust.

Crafting memories, hand in hand,
Echoes linger in this sacred land.
Foundations strong, we stand so tall,
Within these structures, we heed the call.

Through seasons changing, we will stay,
In gentle silence, we find our way.
A tapestry of love we weave,
In every heartbeat, we believe.

Tides of Time

Waves that crash upon the shore,
Whispers of change, forevermore.
Moments shift like sands that slide,
In each heartbeat, the ocean's pride.

Days grow long, then fade to night,
Stars awaken, a guiding light.
Currents dance with stories old,
Tides of time, a tale retold.

Footprints vanish with the tide,
Yet memories, they still abide.
Turning pages, waves will rise,
In every sunset, truth belies.

As time flows on, we learn to sail,
Navigating dreams, we will not fail.
In every ebb, in every flow,
We'll find our way, as rivers grow.

Fragmented Echoes

Whispers linger in the night,
Thoughts like shadows take their flight.
Memories dance in fractured light,
Echoes fade before the sight.

Silent stories drift away,
They once shone, now dull and gray.
Fragments lost in dull dismay,
Echoes of a brighter day.

Reflections trapped in glassy tears,
A past enchained by hidden fears.
In stillness, time ever nears,
Fragmented whispers, soft and clear.

Yet through the cracks, a spark can gleam,
As twilight weaves its fragile dream.
Hope emerges from the seam,
In tearing silence, we still beam.

Anchors in Turbulent Waters

Beneath the waves, the anchors sway,
In tempest storms, they hold their stay.
Through restless tides, they find their way,
Guiding lost souls who drift astray.

The ocean roars with fury bright,
Yet anchors whisper, 'Hold on tight.'
In churning depths, they shine with light,
Steadfast in shadows, brave the fight.

Each gust of wind and tidal pull,
Tests of strength, yet hearts are full.
The journey seems so vast and cruel,
But love remains the constant rule.

Through waves of change and shifting sand,
Anchors hold with gentle hand.
In every storm, a union planned,
Together strong, we make our stand.

Mirrors in the Soil

Beneath the earth, secrets lie,
Reflections of a world gone by.
Roots entwined, whispers call,
Nature's canvas, a hidden thrall.

Time drips slow in shadowed glades,
Fingers dance through twilight shades.
Every grain holds ancient tales,
Silent stories in the veils.

In darkness deep, the truths ignite,
Shimmering dreams in the soft twilight.
Seeds of hope in the deep reside,
Growing visions, a silent guide.

When misty mornings break the spell,
Mirrors gleam where spirits dwell.
Life and death, a perfect fold,
In mirrors deep, the soil holds gold.

Beneath the Boughs of Memory

In the shade where shadows play,
Time meanders, slow and gray.
Branches cradle dreams of old,
Stories whispered, softly told.

Leaves like pages, turned with care,
Carrying scents of summer air.
Moments linger, frail yet bright,
As echoes dance to fading light.

Roots embrace the earth so tight,
Carving pathways in the night.
Beneath the boughs, the heartbeats sound,
Where fragments of the past are found.

In twilight's hush, reflections gleam,
A tapestry of love's sweet dream.
Beneath the boughs, we find our place,
In nature's arms, a warm embrace.

Milton Keynes UK
Ingram Content Group UK Ltd.
UKHW021858151124
451262UK00014B/1326